CAGE OF LIT GLASS

CAGE OF LIT GLASS

WINNER OF THE 2018 AUTUMN HOUSE POETRY PRIZE **CHARLES KELL**

AUTUMN
HOUSE PRESS
PITTSBURGH, PA

"Autumn House Press" and "Autumn House" are registered trademarks owned by Autumn House Press, a nonprofit corporation whose mission is the publication and promotion of poetry and other fine literature.

Autumn House Press receives state arts funding support through a grant from the Pennsylvania Council on the Arts, a state agency funded by the Commonwealth of Pennsylvania, and the National Endowment for the Arts, a federal agency.

Cover Image: *Study for Self-Portrait, 1982* by Francis Bacon
© The Estate of Francis Bacon. All rights reserved, DACS, London / ARS, NY / Artimage 2018. Photo: Prudence Cuming Associates Ltd.

Book design by Tyler Crumrine

ISBN: 978-1-938769-39-9
LCCN: 2019933576

All Autumn House books are printed on acid-free paper and meet the international standards of permanent books intended for purchase by libraries.

for Peter Covino

Table of Contents

1.   Enclosures

2.   In a Field

3. Exculpate

4. False Requiem

Enclosures

We must learn to read
In the dark

—John Ashbery

In the Penal Colony

The bucket job is mine.
Sopping up muck,
cleaning mop strings.

They give me extra: bits
of brown paper,
plastic ring to hold a letter

from two years ago. They
give me a softened piece
of wax to plug my ears against

the din. Rattling bars, I still hear
the beating of hard metal
against a concrete wall. A traveler

might wander down the wrong
road and end up here. He can
have the top bunk. He can have

my mop. I will give him a name,
show him where to begin,
show him how to put the wax in.

Rorschach Test

Blink if you see a pain-devil.
Make a left fist if you notice your ma
slicing bread. Wipe the wet
when you make out your dead father.
Black morphs into blue shadows who ring
themselves around your heart handle.
Your first girl's red hair.
Third boy's bruise.
There, see a football floating off
the edge of a cliff.
Tap your right toe twice if you catch
a river swallowing a lost boy.
Your childhood dog, Bear,
wagging its black tail.
The Amish man who cut his finger off.
Close your eyes if you can see your jail cell.
Sit up straight if you see the sawmill.
Open your eyes if you can.

Rimbaud

How the doors of the stone
house bang forever, never shut.
Ruined in a month. In a bare
white room where the sun
inches through the broken window.
How withdrawal and abjection
stun my body, skin crawling
like the rusted back teeth
of an old handsaw. How Rimbaud
ran through the jungle at night, seeing
all, vines smacking his cheeks
while leeches housed
and sucked underneath his wet
clinging pants. Forgotten black
hyacinth. My mother wrote me
the same letter for a year while
I was trapped in Lorain, Ohio, wearing
an issued blue uniform. She said
I am getting old.
She said the house is falling.
The walls move, she said, in the middle
of the night, and I swear I
put the lamp there then it was gone.
I write to no one:
I made it out alive, finally. The walls
either move or sit still, always where
they're supposed to be. I sing
quietly in the leech-black night. Running
and running, like Rimbaud, eyes wide
open, everything in front of me.

Cenotaph

There is a phenomenon amongst
former prisoners where after release
they begin to reconstruct the very
dimensions of the cell they once
were housed in. A rip inside where
the action ends then begins. A clock
is drawn with graphite. A window
is carved, then on top of it the limb
from a tree. Thousands of books out
of nowhere. A pencil and sheets of
white paper. With skinny arms

walls are lined with wet, gray matter.

Mark's Death Mask

There was nothing of what we
talked about written there. Way
too white. The black whiskers
little bruises just above the mouth
shut like a question mark. Flashes
make the lines fade. I wonder if his
eyes are there staring into the back
of his closed eyelids. Bulging
cotton balls after the blood is sucked
out. Everything in the world is eaten
away. He looks horrible. Dying
again waiting to be buried.
My reflection from his wax face is a black
box. His eyes are sewed shut. His eyes
are no longer there. They remain
trapped in the tree he crashed into
wide open on Vair Road. He has run
away. He is gone, trapped
at last in one spot.

Bodybuilder

He takes a fresh razor
presses gently to his chest
staring dead-straight in the mirror.

Cock in left hand, terror
head, vanilla protein powder
crusted yellow on the kitchen counter.

Ninety-five-pound dumbbells on an incline
bench alone in a fluorescent
basement. My body sweats.

My body gorges with blood,
wide veins press my biceps. Wet breath.
In the mirror I see another.

Fresh razor glides under
arms, blindly scrapes the back
of thighs. Mouth open.

I can become something else.
Take my eyes outside, let them float
overhead. Watch me move,

feel another body press against.
Be a total stranger. My body is mostly
water. Blood drip from a soft razor

prick. Semen seeps through the tip
of my gym shorts. Coming toward
every image you think you see

—almost there—staring back at me.

Empty Specter

A fifth of Maker's Mark and some blow burns as we pass
over; blood blooms in Lichtenberg figures on the smashed window
making me want to scream but my mouth fills with glass.

Debris piles, charred car parts in a field of verdigris; gas
drips down, arms tremble out the door—like a TV show,
blow mixed with a fifth of Maker's Mark burns passing

over everything undulates; faces erased by happening fast,
"I'm still alive" met with burnt ash; a doppler of blood flow
makes me want to scream, but when I open my mouth fills with glass

shards wreathed around Mark's body, lying for the last
time next to me. Destruction in the present tense—an accident. Slow
burn from a bottle of bourbon, cocaine cut with levamisole, we pass

out in a dark roll, smoke rises, a dream, a blast
that causes a storm of bones, tendrils of metal, faces lying in snow,
I want to scream but my open mouth fills with glass;

the spider-webbed windshield, we no longer recall the ghost cast
shadows over this mausoleumed Jeep Cherokee. All the blow;
a fifth of Maker's Mark on Vair Road burns as we pass
over and it makes me want to scream but my mouth is full of glass.

Two Weeks Inside a Locked Attic

On day one I stare into a mirror through a blanket of dust.

On day two I realize the door doesn't open.

On day three I masturbate to a photo I find of an old classmate.

On day four I laugh hysterically while my arms reach out.

On day five I weep into a dirty sheet.

On day six I capture a mouse and name it Franz Schubert.

On day seven I think of the people I have hurt.

Day eight: I see a torn shirt with the faint visage of Elvis Presley (I leave it be).

On day nine I build a city from an olio of leaves I find in the corner.

On day ten I eat Franz Schubert.

On day eleven I scratch out a message on the floor with a rusty nail.

Day twelve: I wonder if those noises are real.

On day thirteen my breath makes smoke rings that rise then disappear.

On day fourteen I can't remember why I'm here.

The Trial

Judge said last time I skipped
bail but it was a lie.
Labeled "flight risk" among many
other things. Say, is the sky
behind me still? Pretty the way snow
falls then rests on the barbed
wire fence.

Shallow breath of others next to me.
Rhapsody of locks, steps in time.
You spoke of needing me once.
Asking if I would come & I did:
car sped through nine hours of ice.
I need you now.
They want to put me somewhere

I don't want to go.

In a Dark Room

I see him when I close my eyes,
splayed out on a table disguised

as a bed, piss dribbles into a bag,
a fly lands on the oxygen machine.

I never meant what I said or thought,
really. It's silly to call time a linear

palimpsest; an imposture, more
matter-of-factly, more use out

of the plain lie, glass surfaces
is how I describe his eyes,

more surfaces meant to defend
against depths. Your room, now

a charnel house where you self
flay until you waste away to

nothing. The gnaw
at your entrails until you're

eventually strangled by your bowels.
(Once you burnt all your records

in a rust-orange oil drum.)
Another act of empty atonement:

to compose an epic of silence.
Finally, in stillness, your slow death slog.

House Arrest

Unplug it from the wall
then quickly back in.

The phone rings.
I'm attached, plugged-

in while the wall
seems to move. Thirty-two

steps. The phone rings.
I quickly plug it back

in again. It senses through
my skin. I hold the bottle

over Mother's head
ready to strike but instead

hit mine over & again
until blood runs down.

Next morning I unplug
it, Mother drives me

to turn it in & I am gone not
to be seen for a long time.

Self-Portrait as Invisible Being

Climb three rails at once.
The way to cut fog with a silver
        finger.
My key says stop. Says Descartes
the comedian laughed all the way
to the scaffold. His nose
got lost in the shadows. Here
I am ruffling the basket's wooden
stalks. Hidden under my bed
all alone. This is a telephone, a flower
epistle, a passenger pigeon,
a cruise missile. This pencil pestle
        & mortar.
My underside whistles when I walk
by. Or else you couldn't see me if
you tried. The way I sit still for days
is a reckless act.

Janitor Hiding in a Locked Closet

This switch pulls the strips tight.
Carved Li Po on the back of my left
    wrist.
Could teach you these anatomies in the dark.
Could tell you about certain Eastern
poets who've died surrounded by millions
of tiny worms spinning silk.

Read these things: how to paint the sky
after a hurricane; how to untie four
hundred different knots; the perfect fold.
Rustle out away from here, adjacent
    corridor.
Wet wax basketball glides by my door.

I worked for this family made of thick
skin & rock. In this school met Tim
who has an owl's head. I was a painter once,
cupped a candle in cobalt blue, spread its X
across lunchroom walls for you.

Lincoln Town Car

After you hit Rob in the face
I tackled you & trapped, you
crushed your lips against mine.

Earlier that night, in your
maroon Lincoln Town Car,
you smashed Dave's father's

antique Corvette parked with
a tarp covering it. Your foot
accelerated & your right arm

reversed, laughing until Rob
& I forced you out & he drove
back to the Windham projects.

With a swollen eye, Rob looked
gaped-mouth at our kiss which
was over in a second & never

mentioned again, as if below
sea level we met & our bodies
became tangled until we broke

the surface. Reminds me when
we were twelve & thirteen, how we cut
our arms & licked each other's

blood in a boys' ritual under
stars. Last summer we played
catch with an old football while

your wife looked on, your daughter
joining us & the sickness over
what we've done to our lives

leaves me. The football moves in
a soft arc through the air & I think
back to the summer fifteen years

ago, driving in your Lincoln Town
Car with open beers & a joint, how
you wrapped your arms around

my body that one night after
smashing the Corvette & punching
Rob in the face, how a few days

later you touched my shoulder
& stared into my eyes, thanking me
for the 350 dollars for an abortion

you didn't want your girl to have.

Enclosures

Into four stone walls, a physical
manifestation of my *mens rea*. More
precisely, a copy of a copy of no copy.
Where silver ingots break into gray rivulets
and fugue down. You can conjecture on
physical ways out, or concentrate on the window:
rhododendron forests; an ochre rooftop; a tip of a tree
branch in a phthalo field. Both a part and

apart. Or to try to speak into a void (sort
of an improvisational hacking away at time).
Or to look in the mirror and see an empty face.
Or to keep moving forward and backward—slowly
and even slower yet, taking interstitial
steps—as if there is no place.

Vetiver

Inside my fist wet grass makes a soft sound.

Eyes Composed of Fine Particles That Drift Away

1.

He watches me bounce a ball
on a ground of quartzite pebbles,
     then shoot the ball.

 He's not really watching me.
 He stares through my body
 as the ball bounces, echoes
     ricochet off the rocks—
     then float away.

  (His eyes are Desiderius Erasmus.
  His eyes are "Ah, Bartleby!"
  His eyes are: Daddy's not home on Christmas.)

 The voice on the pay phone
 sounds like the drift of sand.
 What scares me the most is me.
 Only the automated voice is audible: "you
     have one minute remaining."

2.

Traces of him appear out of nowhere:
he sits on a picnic table watching me.

I am not frightened of being alone.
The cop pulls us over, he says: "go,
     run inside the house."

His eyes are:
  a) Lake Okeechobees
  b) Tired country singers (Haggard looking Merles)
  c) Zeno's paradoxes
  d) All of the above
  e) None of the above

He sits in front of a blank wall,
like a glassy lake with minute
      particles of debris floating
      on top.
(He now makes) music like a muzzle of bees.

My eyes are Arshile Gorkys.
The only thing that frightens me is me.

3.

He really watches the other boy
while he pretends to watch me.
(The one he never talks about, the
one he never tells anyone about).
The cops pull me over and say:
        "put your hands on the car;
        spread your legs; place your
        hands behind your back, wrists together."

A discursive assemblage consists of strands and
segments of prose that connect and reconnect.

Mother cries.
She doesn't believe what she finds.

I scare easily.
I open the door—it's me.

His eyes are: "do not resuscitate." His
eyes are simultaneous eternities. His eyes
are prisms of plastic. His eyes are black
glass. His eyes are forty-seven
wings. Echo chambers.

4.

Another multiform enclosure collapses.
Places thought safe are the exact opposite.
Days are numbers here.
Words describing eyes written in a book
        of glass rise then disappear.

I can't see the way I used to see.
I'm in a gray room lined with acoustic panels—

I think of you like a hinge—you were never
there. The ball bounces in order to
replicate the sound of a metronome.

His eyes are mechanisms of concealment.
His eyes are a sea of invisibilities.
Starving philosophers.

First we build the circular walls with flecks of metal.
Windows are parallelograms that look out.
The only way up is to climb a rope
of sand. The mirror erases our faces. I draw
your outline in a book of glass. If you ever bang
this door down, you will find no one inside.

In a Field

like the phantom beat between two rhythms

—Rosmarie Waldrop

Two Fields

1.

In a strange field never
entered. Here once, though
    I can't remember when.

2.

In a strange field never
entered. Here once, though
    I can't remember when.

Sciosophy

In a mirror another mirror.
    My secret isn't safe with me.

I can never imagine what it's like not
    to want. October, alone, in

the context of one's surroundings:
    the brown table, book-

cases heavy with dust,
    flicker of the lit orange

candle. A wasp on the screen,
    ghost shoes on my feet—

not going anywhere. Words
    never what I need them to.

A boy, my friend at sixteen,
    running together in a shallow

creek bed outside Nelson's
    Ledges as the hail bruises

our backs. He is waiting
    there, ahead without turning

around. He's now a wreck with-
    out a helmet. Twisted pieces

of metal and blood on
    the pavement. All of this you

know until now. Skin traces.

Welcome Snow

You don't really know
what is happening. I want
you to bash my face in until—
unrecognizable—my teeth
lie on the ice and blood

pours into the cracks
of the sidewalk. We hear
the snow fall on our roof.
A scalding cup.
I can will sickness away

by concentrating on a certain
crack in the corner
of the kitchen's ceiling. When
I turn eighteen again I will
join the marines in order

to go AWOL. Peel off
my burning skin and run
into the wood. Build a fire and sleep
with my eyes open.
When they come for me

I'll be waiting. I'll bite the first
man who grabs me. My teeth
will make a sound like a bomb
until all run away and I'm alone, wild.

The Lost Boy

I.   Film

Sister is sick, puking
up food on purpose, everyone
gone, "wings of a fly"
caught in her throat "on fire."

Huddle together, we walk the white goat down
Freedom Road in Ohio.
My name is Dirt: nine years old.
The stars reach out to grab one another

then blow up. Cold
pieces of dirt rain down.
We watched *The Lost Boys* over & over.
Popcorn,

Pepsi. Sno-Caps. "They're maggots
Michael. How are those worms,
Michael?" In her throat burns
acid from wretched food. "I'm all right"

she says. All that is required is emptied
out. A little farewell.
When I was older I got sent
to jail, and Sister disappears.

I have to find her. I swear on all
the salt floating in the air. She is here,
somewhere in the city. Bits of
red string, loose strands of her hair.

II.   Novel

In *Pedro Páramo* ideas are stones.
The cantina is lit with burning flies.

A gambler in the distance holds a broken guitar.
Cut thumbs are dipped in gasoline to kill bacteria.

Washers dig through bodies for coin.
They hang lungs on the line to dry.

They whistle in the wind at the end of day.
Medicine is chewed leaves.

Bits of glass are used to look behind.
Two hands feel like a dozen.

Quicklime covers the smell.
We stand in the wood speaking low.

The hunted run yet are hungry & slow.
This is our last match.

III.   Memoir: Entropy

Headless statues float in a broken
        open Cornell box, past last call.

In a small room off the water,
        wind burns through empty bottles

making neon green headstones
        that stare back from the windowsill.

Even before your brother died,
        you felt like an only child crawling

in the dark. Under the bed you shared
        for twelve years he built a herbarium,

cigarette butts planted on the periphery
        with faces drawn over them. This

was your family. To lure the stricture
        away, clouds inside the closet, shirts

shrink over your scratched shoulders.

IV.   Painting: Francis Bacon's *The Black Triptychs*

You could talk about the toilet.
Sideways face jutting
    out.

The way hands make claws,
nothing to hold onto.

Face smeared mirror, frozen
    forever.

There, a red spot. Dark city
in the corner.

Sick light bulb, broken eye.
I have been in a place like this.

Seen a man bent over, arms splayed, still.

The stale air inside.
Wooden ship pushed in a bottle

broken sail, broken mast. Favorite
pair of slacks vomit stained. The remains

of a glass of port on the green
coffee table. Red ring. Naked bodies

bent facing in a dimly lit
room. I've lost my sense of direction,

behind closed eyes misery-stars sprinkle.
Oblique creaking.

Forget waves that wash over your body.

Stripped to the waist. Salt clings to your cheeks,
hair on your arms stands straight & still.

The mirror novel walking down the sand. Go,
says the bird. Blue vein spiders his arm.

Go, calls someone far away. You are almost there.

Wristwatch two loops tight. You made it, blue
        tongue

lolls. Someone found you this way—not me—I would
have left your body there. Walked down the road.

Smoked a cigarette under the streetlamp.

V.   The Other Novel

where the boy sings
for hours in the forest alone.

His aching hand claps bark
for each night spent on the ground.

He went looking for his dead sister.
A circus finds him, feeds the hungry

mouth sweet bread, cool liquid drips
down his chin staining a torn shirt.

Stars are clocks floating above
the clockmaker's skin. The boy runs

away to go looking again. Crickets
click *bildungsroman* to the red leaves.

It was stupid, this idea. The boy
agrees. He thinks I can't see him perched

in a tree with bow & arrow pointed
at my lung. In its golden spit, rusty pins.

I rip each page to fine bits, scatter them
on the forest floor where they will

become loam, swamp fisted with insects.

A Hunger Artist

They call him Traveler.
He made this song from nothing:
corrugated window-wire,
scratchy graph. They laugh

at him in the cage, rummaging
through a pile of leaves.
Torn sleeves, debris stains.
They take his name away.

Illuminating, dryly tapping
aperture. He whispers "Traveler,"
recalls his song: "I too can
take away then build upon."

Black bars, warbler's cry.

Close Stranger

Built, torn down, then built
again. A small stone structure
in the middle
of this snowy wasteland.

Where we met & sucked
cold air into our smoke-
burnt lungs. Colder autumn.
Tractor cap off & rag

dipped into gas to start
a small fire. Your scarf
was wet & smelled
like a mix of cinnamon & piss.

Dragging your nails across
my lower back, zeroing in
on what the mind empties out.
I took you there, all evidence

against. Still remember? Cold
no longer cold. Red house far
up the road. Wrecked nausea
a little money took away.

Two sheets tied together, red
too. Dress flat & ripped.
My arms scraped raw by
the almost frozen thorns

poking through the dirt into our skin.

Two Weeks with Don Quixote

1

We ride toward the hill, built fast
from machines braided with many
moving parts. Down the well our arms
wave like wings, catching pebbles
in the crook of the nail. Stick close
to the armor. The nag needs oats.
The princess, he whispers, wears pink

2

underwear. This string stings if tied too tight.
Toward the end he made a constant
clucking sound. He touched my shoulder
while staring straight through the ground.
The sea is wide & vast with many floating colors.
We move our arms quick as if to fly away.
A vast & wide sea owns many floating colors.

The Robber

He took the black
cloak down, walked
back & forth in the cage
of lit glass.

Counted thirteen steps
until the night clock
stopped cold. In the white
wall a crooked crack

seethes & blurs. Give
back your wish treat-
ment. Pariah-complex
caught in a tense fist.

He took your last call,
rain mark, silver wire.
His words are wheels
working to be set free.

Fluorescent Garbage Can

we doused with hair-
spray then set on fire
throwing long matches in. Eye-
brows singed, throats scratchy

why Mark kept spraying
Chloraseptic until he got sick.
He almost drove the four-
wheeler into the pond later

that winter. I tried to ride
but couldn't shift down.
The snowflakes caught my eye-
lids half open. Mark looked

like he was dancing, looked
blessed with antennae as he stood
in the frozen-blue night
playing an invisible guitar,

frame of white sparks glittering
his head, his hands

The Windows

were left open,
door un-
locked. The ice

along the glass
bottom
melts onto

the white carpet.
So, they say,
the next great

philosophy
will be pity
for no one.

A handful
of dust bearing
down over

a poor photo-
graph. The blue
flower whose

name I forget.
The skull
hanging over

the mantel, keys
through two eye-
holes.

The marks
I made
on the wall. Green

then gray.

Guilty

To drink one's self sober
again, abstract way. Doppelgänger,
neon warrior, I live wide
open & ready, like a sick eye.

The city is still strange, the kiss
our names pledged, wet hand
in back pocket. Lost but not caring,
I kept after you, chasing.

Once I awoke in a cell
yet wasn't sure if it was a dream.
My name was called out
& mouth so dry

I couldn't reply. They took my shoes,
jeans & belt, placed my
wallet in a steel box. Blue swarm
before my eyes, river in a quick

glance from the barred window.
I couldn't say if I loved you when you
held me down, writhing. Though
I whispered your name over & after.

Lincoln Town Car

In October 1999, three
months after Mark died,
I bought the light-blue Lincoln,

then later that night cut
my left knee open, high
on Percocet, wrestling with

Nick Reed in a field. Jesse
tore a sleeve to staunch
the blood. I sat laughing

at the pop & swirl from
the fire's sparks. Here's a black
glass skeleton in

the passenger seat. The deserted
playground where we ran
to the top dressed as scarecrows.

I kept a shoebox of cassette
tapes—hear hollow voices
ring. Kept, on my passenger

seat, a branch from the tree
where they wrecked the Jeep
Cherokee. One night I lit

it on fire & held on until
flames licked my wrist. We're buried
animals in the tar

Mark spoke about. I take the Polaroid
of his half-face, place it in
the glove box. I turn the lights off

while I drive down Vair Road.
Touch my scar. Call out dates at will,
collect wind, open my hands

to let go. Nothing happens.

Self-Portrait as Cotard Delusion

Rations are mouthed
& chewed, prisoner fashion.
Each step here measured,
clamped in a book gilded
with ornate gold curl. My hair
grows short. I take blame
for the words of the dead. Remember
what I said? Each night when
you're alone think of my tongue
trilling this bone song. Broken
anchor. Electric wire. The real touch
felt below the thin, fake skin.

Old Piano

It took everything to move it in.
Sideways, on a wheeled cart,
dead-now Steve holding the thing
steady while I carried it, pulled it in
    the corner myself.

Mother was proud—one
broken leg, out of tune.
No one knew how to play.
After I was released from Glenbeigh

I sat on the stool in the summer,
plucking the beginning of a Joplin
rag tune Tony showed me
while I was away. It made me think

of Kate and me walking in the park,
the ice cream truck
driving by. Looking at each other.
She drove away in the middle
    of winter

from our small rented house in Toledo,
Ohio. Tears and snow. Silver Pontiac
Sunfire driving slow over ice
on the turnpike back to Warren.

We were going to give it away.
Donate it. It cost more to tune
than what my mother paid.
I pressed a white key down.

It didn't make a sound.

Felon

One time only
the walls started
to close in. My

head pounded
with sweat, damp
beads on my

arms and thighs.
Dirty white concrete
pressed against

my temples.
It was dark
except for the moon

glowing on barbed
wire curling over
the fence outside

my window.

Exculpate

But it still remains to be said, that Pierre himself had written many a fugitive thing...

—Herman Melville

Wild Turkey

The letter sent in wavy writing which read
"I can no longer shave because my hand shakes."

I didn't return for your funeral, though, I lay
on the burial plot your mother-in-
law bought for you inside the small cemetery
        in Footville, Ohio.

Thanksgiving, before I went away
for a year, which you didn't mention,
        thank you, Tim.

We walk in the middle of the road no
one around. In a faraway field a black

dog runs fast chasing a faster thing. Green
flannel, a cap with flaps covering your ears.

Everyone back at the house waiting for us to eat.
Quiet now—our breath, smoke in the air,

train tracks, frost under our black boots.

Please Free My Dear Friend Jack

He's the most amazing
& already they take him, fate
beautys up the mirror, wonders
how one gets used to tighter.

I wake alone, say Jack
until I lose & the white
of my eyes vibrates & blood
drips in ríos down my nose.

Almost a model, food-
trays slip through the tiny
slit an effort to ingest, down
twenty-five lbs. feeling born again.

They try in every way to reach
you. They flatter, they promise
time they can never give.
In silence you sit not nodding

your head, night pedal
an invisible bike. Day paces.
New larva. Draw a shovel
over your bed. Draw a hole.

Draw a blonde girl wearing
a short skirt. Just enough so you can see
the edge of her white panties.
I move slow fingers over

my hip bones, ribs, skin
so white & clear. Hair (unkempt)
with a pen missing its shell
(so not to hurt) I write

a letter to you then rip it to shreds.
I start over and describe the apples
in my dream. I mention my blonde
girlfriend Lindsay, my fingers forever

moving. Your eyes like two Jupiters
floating over me before I fall off to sleep.

Nineteenth-Century American Literature

Sometimes, in the darkness
when no one is around, I call my penis
Henry Wadsworth Longfellow.

I say "Life is very long."
I say "The meaning of life is that it stops."

Then one summer after the diagnosis
of degenerative discs and spinal
stenosis I drink Bloody Marys
and eat Percocet every day, feeling
self-pity, until I think of a man
I love dying of cancer, wasting away
in a small, book-lined apartment.

Like Pierre Glendinning, I take my Lucy
in disparate spaces: bent over in a dressing
room with her arm twisted behind, winced face
in the mirror, wet smack the only sound
until "oh shadow" escapes from her
mouth. And she ambushes me, straddles
my body and slaps my face—our smiles
a mirror as I lick the blood from my lips.

Gone now, I start to see "mysteries
interpieced with mysteries, and begin
to see the mere imaginariness of
the supposed solidest principle of human
association."

Longfellow's wife burns in a blaze of hot wax.
Rivers of orange flames lick her until all
that remains is a charred husk. He no longer
shaves his beard, the rusty razor lies in a forgotten bucket.

Contemporary preoccupations rearrange
past events. "Whenever I find myself
growing grim about the mouth; when-
ever it is a damp, drizzly November

in my soul; whenever I find myself
involuntarily pausing before coffin ware-
houses, and bringing up the rear of every
funeral I meet..." I walk out to my
back porch at midnight in a tessera
of stillness trying to compose a mosaic
lotus. "This is my substitute for pistol
and ball." Despite my will the body shakes.

The Haruspicator

I comb through air with old bones.
Catch your blonde hair between
teeth. Keep a box of notes
in the trunk of a blue Lincoln Town
     Car.

A father came to his rest in the back
room. A mother's shadow smokes
& walks the floor all night. Nothing
bothers. Only when the ground

cracks open & I must sift through it.
When a body is brought
& I must answer why, moving
my fingers through flesh like a million
     maggots.

When the light inside burns out. I take
the painting of you down from the wall,
make small creases in the blue oil with
a fingernail. This is rain. Half of the word

painting is pain. Pry earth with a crab-
apple branch, use a fork & wire screen
to sweep away. Every rock in the world
is the same. One day you're here then not.

Looking down at the mud is like staring
into a mirror. My hands caked with earth.
The bone, skin, wet fur. Tomorrow
I will walk alone in the forest. Tonight

I sit in the dark drawing this picture.

Pseudobulbar Affect

Tim calls in a lunatic monster,
cries the weather has thrown
damp weeds across his back.
Cries when are you coming home.
Mouth so goddamn squeamish,
electricity fit laughter covers
it in its own way.

I was calling to tell you I love you.
I was calling to hear your voice.
I was calling to conjure your face.
To make the water stop.
I'm calling because I put John Lee Hooker
on & thought of you.

Novel

I am writing a ball of snakes.
Counting & stacking pills

into a sacred monument.
Each chapter will feature

a body writhing in pleasure
under blue fluorescent.

Pills mixed with tea
make a transparent ink.

The wood will have disco balls
hanging from stiletto branches.

Snakes lunge at the wall,
crawling into gray crevices to escape.

Threnody

Mike drops his tinfoil pipe
then fires his gun in the air.
Eleven years since his little
brother Ryan died, the doctor

drilling holes in his head
to release the swelling caused
from meth. I missed the funeral—
too busy in Chicago drinking

coffee, walking over the city
streets. I knock now on Mike's
trailer door down a side
lane they call heroin alley.

Gaunt, he invites me in and hands
me a beer I drink slow
in the dim living room,
enjoying our time together.

Mike sold us a shitty chunk
of heroin for sixty bucks a year
ago and Luke was pissed though
I didn't care. We stare at the dirty

carpet taking slow sips. Ryan
died, Mike fell into a deep
black hole—stealing jewelry, money
from his mother in order to stay

in habit, as they say. The snow melts
on the porch into a black puddle
as I sit on the couch thinking about
Mike's brother, ask him for another.

Exculpate

He asked the man to let him go.
The man said no.
He asked for a bowl,
a drink of water.
He stood straight, iron bar
face melting.

Arm caught once, tore it out,
away, the mark like animal
scrapes. Aluminum
taste in a mouth.

Tried it with his hands tied
behind his back. Counted all
the times he wouldn't go back.
With feet bound, eyes
                                closed.

Count the dots on the ceiling.
He asked him one last time
before the bomb.
At last, he can say, wrong.
Places created,
each mark on the table.

Parole. Gray ice. Oblivion.

Repeat Offender

Red dots on
your upper left
arm raw from scratching.

Again, this old architecture
sutures you in: spring bed,
metal toilet, dry spit

on the wall, newspaper bits
stuck into window holes.
Lines of sound wrap

around each side you're on.
See this face in the mirror—
how one offers a self

up until one's gone. Wet
pastels. You said never
again. Pretend, stand

somewhere different. There,
take two steps now don't
move for five minutes.

Say never again.

Sarasota Affidavit

1.
Gulls flock
at shifting
detritus.

A layer
peels away.

Over heavy waters,
curlicues

of smoke
drift
into

men who make
war-noises
with their throats.

2.
I laugh when I'm scared.

At the moment
of horrible
disaster

people gather
in groups.

"Cease-fire" written
on everyone's face.

3.
Listen.
The sound
of scissors
cutting

paper is coming
from over there.

Our leaking
faucet sounds
like a water-
fall.

Footsteps
like a mouse
climbing out from
an oubliette.

Our laughter is the sound of sex.

4.
I'm kept by
a shadow with
no name.

It uses me as bait.

It makes me
the creator
of a new kind
of hate.

It makes
me dig
tiny rows
in the garden
with a tiny
hoe.

What for
I don't know.

5.
He
disappears
before our eyes.

Every law
we've ever broken
is recorded

on a cheap
sheaf
of papers

locked away
in an ancient
wooden desk.

Heaven used
to be a weight
room. Our bed.
That one bar.
My wrecked
Town Car.

I don't believe in hell.

My last name
rhymes
with jail cell.

Felon

My wife says I am cold.
That my heart
is made from burnt blue steel.

Back in Warren, I drive
a black Pontiac down a long
dirt road past a falling gray

house. I wonder who
lives there, if he is happy.
In a field behind the house

are trees. Hidden in the trees
is a shed. I creep into this shed,
sit down on the ground

and become someone else.

Father's Small Box

sits on her bedroom shelf, discreet.
I wait until she leaves, tiptoe
back & open the top, lick
my left pinkie then dip it in.
Place the inchoate gray
smudge in my mouth, swirl
the soft, wet paste then swallow hard.

Monsieur Robber

He's as master-
ful a wine drinker
as Sancho Panza.

Caught flat,
whispering in a garden
of secrets.

Tied the wrong key
around his neck
with a quick string.

Kept the lawn
girl waiting, rag-
amuffin, sing-

ing a tunnel
in the sky. The tea-
pot comes two

days late. Tug-o-
war with
a river demon.

He chases her
outstretched & far
across the moat.

In a Dark Room

Alone in a house at night
she has been drinking for days,
crying on the phone, my mother
screams words I can't make out.

She has been drinking for days.
"Why aren't you here helping me,"
she screams these words I refuse to make out.
But I know what she says, and say nothing back.

(Why are you not here helping me).
In the invisible mirror stands a ghost,
but I know who it is and say nothing back.
She talked to me while I sat in jail,

the invisible mirror stares a ghost.
Three years ago I swore all would change.
She talked to me while away.
Pretended to listen, to be there for her.

Years ago I said all this would change.
Both of us almost the same.
She talked to me while I was locked away,
and I promised to always be there for her.

I swore all this would change.
Drinking alone in a house at night,
pretending to listen.
Crying on the phone, my mother.

Self-Portrait with Hands Made of Wire

He's kept behind a fence.
After being fed, lie back down
on scratchy metal. Coils
are nodes he uses to make noise.
The sound of wire on concrete
trying to get out. The sound of feet
padding back and forth over the floor.
There is a wave inside a steel box he can carry.
You can't hear the water rushing.
Can only see the salt rusting his hands away.

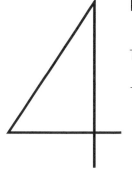

False Requiem

This is Avignon? That's how his Avignon is.

—Daniël Robberechts

The Carcasser

is what Marc called me, drinking
Bushmills in the Time Out bar,
when he said "you are a thing which picks
at the bodies of both living & dead."

Carcassing: taking a person's body
& representing it to fit one's needs.
Ripping it open & then sticking
a pencil in the ribs to dig around.

Marc laughed. Then he read my story
of us, after we left the bar in Garrettsville.
Speechless, he stared out the window as
we drove down Mumford Road.

I gather stones & stack them on each other.
My wife hasn't spoken in weeks.

Bandit Hand

Grab the grackle's wet
wing festering in the lemon

twilight. I'll dip this lit
finger in the flood

& sign the court document. In
our shrinking backyard stands

the falling swing set
where we held AA meetings.

I stole the word, our record.
Slid the secret note saying what

I heard in the rusted weft
of the oval tube. We stood

in a circle—a wheel inside
of the air, like the wheel that took

the prophet Ezekiel—discussing
night crimes. Condemned sliver,

gnarled knuckle. Let go finally of
everything you clutched & tried

to drag to the bottom of the sea.
Looking low with slit eye sockets

I see white Christmas lights
strung around your head shine

like phosphorus in the night.

Vetiver

We pull up earth with fists like razor
    amulets.

You say "Kell, I keep having this dream
where I'm walking through Byzantium
    decked out

in gold lamé, a sombrero, hungry as hell,
yet when I go to eat my muffin, the blue-
    berries dissolve into

black ants, sand crumbs fleck my beard,
and when I wake

my boxers are wet with semen."

I ignore him. Flat on my back with my eyes
agog. Handfuls of wet grass stream
    from my mouth.

The sky's on fire. Mark is laughing
with his eyes closed, rivers burn

down his cheeks. My silver Buick Century
is parked somewhere over the hill. We've
    been lost

in this cemetery for hours, bathing

in the grass, touching one another.
The sun slowly turns down, leaves move
    like lazy detectives.

Mark's eyes are Byzantium. My hands
are tired and green from clutching at

the grass, letting it fall through my fingers where
    it floats away in the air.

Daguerreotype

He had a way of saying
the truth—all at once
—in a walking barefoot

over broken glass style.
His wish for death
these fifteen long years

finally here. Thought
I was prepared. The constant
practice of slowly shutting

him out: the twice-a-year visits
whittled down to one then none
(the never-replied-to texts

it horrifies me now to admit).
How, the last time ever
his broken black truck

parked outside of the Time
Out bar—(our bar)—I drove
by without looking back.

Cleaning out my boyhood
room in Ohio after my mother
was gone I found a photo of him

and me one month after the wreck
in July 1999. My arm is around
his neck—his eyes stare straight

ahead wishing to forget everything
in the world. A tattered Wheeler
Landscaping polo covers him

while I wear a *Bridges to Babylon*
Rolling Stones concert T-shirt.
I want to describe the look on my

face as hurt yet cannot. I thought
everything would one day
get better after all of our prisons.

It never did. My mother told
me while I was away Marc
offered to send money.

"I owe him" he said "for all
the money he sent me" while
Marc was trapped for four

long years at the Lake Erie
Correctional Institution.
Here is this photo I'm holding

now. Edges brown, worn down,
my arm wrapped tightly around
Marc's back, never letting go.

My Alcoholic Other

waits in the recovery room
in North East Ohio while sick

Lake Erie froths damp
onto the bitten edges of the city.

I poured him a glass of scorpions.
Kept the mirror notes written,

transcendental, blue bird, naked as Thoreau.
Told the true lie why I left run-

ning that one night while the red
lights chased you down the alley.

I was running with you, not from you, see.
I meant to say I tried to call, to give

up, poured the last bottle down
a blue drain. There's the final cup.

The glued hole in the wall filling with shadow.
The last pain felt, you no longer you.

Wet Cigarette

Plays a role. Landscapes the presence of.
Far enough too far extension: afraid

of the track, lost bobbin at sea. Pair of ripped

jeans, half-unbuttoned half-untucked shirt.
Black centipede moves across the bar, andante.

Oh how it burns oh sigh tiger-man. Tonight

play a movie the one with his hair slicked back
an actor at first familiar then as the film continues

recedes further from view. Faces blur.

The suburbs covered in sand. Say lips pursed
in sadness say I'll see you there tomorrow

say we'll wrap our arms around bodies and say

Tower of Birds

In a blue garden
where heat beads gather
on the bridge

we watch a gray heron
stand at the edge of
a waterfall trying to

collect fish.
Beetles sleep in the shade.
Three white swans

circle the middle
of the murky pond before
slipping into

the small island.
The sun heats my skin,
setting my hands on fire.

The back of my neck
is wet. I don't care—
I can sing about burning.

The art show is soon.
A clown twisting
balloons. I am made

of earth, cool
moss covers bare feet.
Carrie sits next to me.

I touch the pink ring
on her finger.
The girl who will be

my wife looks off into
the distance at a world
I don't yet know.

A Cell the Shape of a Ring

does not really exist. Each one
with four tight corners stuck
fast with dust. Dirt-rot yellow,
spider skeleton bone still under
fluorescent. Opens into an oval
when you're alone, walking in slow
circles. There is a way rats feel,
chewing aluminum foil, running
over a water-wheel. Garbage night
sits heavy, never dark enough for deep
sleep. Touch your ring now. Imagine
moving around it for hours. The bag
over your face goes in and out until

the brown paper gets stuck in your mouth.

Drowning in a Shallow Creek Bed

Another new drug burns its way
through our blood. Glass floats
on the marsh-water. Craig drank
a beer with cigarette butts, words
ashy and garbled. There is the sound
ice makes being crunched between
your teeth. The windchill feeling
burns like a repeated mirror. Mark
is gone and I can't stop thinking about him.

One morning, he said—the sound of his
voice was the sound of a boy speaking
underwater—there will be a place we
can stay, there will be light, people talking,
all of the air in the world is ours. Quartz
rock underfoot. Bits of broken shells.
The hand examines a blue bottle floating
in the water. His name is written on every
page of this book. The book is sinking
to the bottom of the lake.

False Requiem

Mother is still here, alive.
Smoking and drinking alone

in an old red house in Ohio.
I continually prepare for that day,

hope it will be quick, painless.
No protracted agony, no

long, drawn-out wasting away.
No talk with my sister about placing

her somewhere else. I lie a great
deal. List things, excavate spaces.

Make up stories to keep
the ghosts away, and to also draw

them near. Believing the whole
time that all of this is useless. She

was the one—no one else—who drove
to pick me up upon my release

from Lorain, Ohio in 2007.
This sickens me and I hate myself.

Lost Friend

He left his hat over
there on the window-
sill. The rusty door
creaks when closed. What
about the garage, behind
the wooden ladder, in the corner
covered in oily rags?
Without meaning a pipe bursts,
a dry crack starts to run along
the wall. It was different
the last time, less words.
On the table rests an old
newspaper. He crossed over somewhere.
He poured kerosene on his shadow.
There, a flat white guitar pick,
a nondescript bird flying. Its feathers
covered in ice. Over & over
it's flying. Look closely.

Oblivion Letter

Recall a bottle on the table by the window.
Later, running sweaty in the wood,

heels bleeding through brown leather shoes.
If I could taste your cold elixir rush

down my throat once again.
Dear K: the cracked city street has a name

you can whisper. Dark corners to go
looking for anything to feel.

The boy called Night advancing. Green
serpent coils with a mouth of stone.

Burnt plastic smoke scalds finger & lung.
Words you write when your shadow arrives.

I slept in the library, head pressed in a French
poet's biography. I lay cinder strait

in a station basement. Electric trains whipped
by as my open mouth hummed a white cell

sonata. There was almost always more time.
The autumn fields were set on fire, to warm

the dying as they rose, I read in a book. Give
this note an open home. Give the sparkling

dots behind closed eyes names of old friends.
Move slow through stillness. No longer

caress your small devil's alveoli. Starve
the animal inside a little at a time. Think of torn

feet running over dry leaves, twigs.
Hunched in a different city, loose stone, rubble.

Pleiades scars cicatrized on bare
backs. Sewing a torn sleeve with a mid-

night needle. Sewing slivers of mirror
on spotted cotton. Petting blood blisters

with strands of brown hair. The aluminum foil sky over-
head. Bells ringing somewhere. Soft sound of sirens.

Reading in the Dark

1.

Crouched, he takes a book then props
his back against the metal bowl.

The sound of men banging on bars.
Every other page ripped out, used, or thrown
     away.

When the lights come on it is another day.

2.

Slant of fluorescent light
on the growing edge of the toilet.

A ghost card. Apocrypha.

Far Village

The only job is sweeping dirt
over empty streets.
I left my keys there.
Wanted a drink & was handed a glass
    of rocks.
The women carry sick birds in paper bags.
The men are scarecrows with ragged clothes.
I wanted a room & was pointed toward
    a broom closet.
There is no white paper.
I must write on the back of stolen burnt bark.
No one eats meat. There isn't any.
A cold thick paste is leavened
into bowls twice a day.
My body is growing used to it.
The sky is always gray.
I could tell you in past & present
    tense
about the bathing hole. How we slather
our bodies with fetid mud to ward
off insects. My skin grows hard.
I am seeing things.
Figuring things out.
The world is nothing. We sit at a rickety
table, our small bowls in front, waiting.

Acknowledgments:

My thanks to Kimiko Hahn for choosing this manuscript.

My deep gratitude to Timothy Liu for friendship, time, and help.

Thanks to Christine Stroud for care and attention.

My thanks, again and always, to Peter Covino, for everything.

My thanks also to Sandra Kell, Charles Kell (1938-2013), Lisa Galati, Tim Queen, Marcus Tirabasso, Andrew Field, Sara Lundquist, Rob Seton, and Lucas Morrison.

All the love in the world to my wife, Carrie.

Grateful acknowledgment is made to the journals where some of these poems first appeared:

The American Journal of Poetry, Anima (UK), Brickplight, Chariton, Drunk Monkeys, Easy Street, Eunoia, floor_plan_journal, Former People, FRiGG, Frontier, Ghost City Review, Golden Walkman, Gloom Cupboard, IthacaLit, Kestrel, Lingerpost, The Manhattanville Review, New Orleans Review, Pantheon Magazine, Pennsylvania English, The Pinch, Poydras Review, Red Flag Poetry, Red Savina Review, River River Review, Steel Toe Review, Stoneboat, Southward Journal, Work Journal.

Notes:

"We must learn to read / in the dark" is from John Ashbery's poem "Litany" from *As We Know* (1979).

"like the phantom beat between two rhythms" is from Rosmarie Waldrop's *The Reproduction of Profiles* (1987).

"But it still remains to be said, that Pierre himself had written many a fugitive thing..." is Herman Melville's from *Pierre; or, The Ambiguities* (1852).

"This is Avignon? That's how his Avignon is," is from the Daniël Robberechts book *Arriving in Avignon: A Record*, originally published in 1970 in Flemish as *Aankomen in Avignon* and translated in 2010 by Paul Vincent.

"Life is very long," is from T.S. Eliot's "The Hollow Men" from *Poems: 1909-1925* (1925).

"The meaning of life is that it stops." This is the famous quote by Franz Kafka.

"Whenever I find myself growing grim about the mouth; whenever it is a damp, drizzly November in my soul; whenever I find myself involuntarily pausing before coffin warehouses, and bringing up the rear of every funeral I meet.... This is my substitute for pistol and ball," is from Herman Melville's *Moby-Dick; or, The Whale* (1851).

"Oblivion Letter" owes a debt to Richard McCann's *Ghost Letters* (1994).

Charles Kell has poetry and fiction in the *New Orleans Review*, *The Saint Ann's Review*, *Kestrel*, *Columbia Journal*, *The Pinch*, and elsewhere. He is Assistant Professor of English at Community College of Rhode Island's Flanagan campus and associate editor of *The Ocean State Review*. He recently completed a PhD at the University of Rhode Island with a dissertation on experimental writing, criminality, and transgression in the work of James Baldwin, Rosmarie Waldrop, Joanna Scott, and C.D. Wright.

New and Forthcoming Releases:

Cage of Lit Glass by Charles Kell
Winner of the 2018 Autumn House Poetry Prize
selected by Kimiko Hahn

Not Dead Yet and Other Stories by Hadley Moore
Winner of the 2018 Autumn House Fiction Prize
selected by Dana Johnson

Limited by Body Habitus: An American Fat Story
by Jennifer Renee Blevins
Winner of the 2018 Autumn House Nonfiction Prize
selected by Daisy Hernández

Belief Is Its Own Kind of Truth, Maybe by Lori Jakiela

Epithalamia by Erinn Batykefer
Winner of the 2018 Autumn House Chapbook Prize
selected by Gerry LaFemina

Fire and Rain: New and Selected Poems by Patricia Jabbeh Wesley

Heartland Calamitous by Michael Credico

Voice Message by Katherine Barrett Swett
Winner of the 2019 Donald Justice Poetry Prize
selected by Erica Dawson

The Gutter Spread Guide to Prayer by Eric Tran
Winner of the 2019 Rising Writer Prize
selected by Stacey Waite

AUTUMN
HOUSE PRESS

For our full catalog please visit: http://www.autumnhouse.org